The Gene Pool

by
Christi Stewart-Brown

© 1996 Christi Stewart-Brown

The Gene Pool

CAST OF CHARACTERS:

CLAIRE GRAY, 40s, a veterinarian

MIRA GRAY, 40s, a housewife, Claire's lover of twenty-something years

PETER GRAY, 17/18, their only child

PAIGE, 18, Peter's girlfriend

HAROLD CARTER, late-30s, the sperm donor

SETTING
The living room of the Grays' home.

TIME
The present.

Production History:

* Over Our Head Players, Racine, WI; 2002
* Unicorn Theatre, Kansas City, MO; 2001
* Waterfront Playhouse, Key West, FL; 1999
* Phoenix Theatre, Indianapolis, IN; 1999
* Borderlands Theatre, Tucson, AZ; 1999
* Kitchen Theatre, Ithaca, NY; 1999
* Mixed Blood Theatre Company, Minneapolis, MN; 1998
* Woolly Mammoth Theatre Company, Washington DC; 19
* Staged Reading, New York Theatre Workshop, New York, NY; 1996

1999 Helen Hayes Award Nomination for Outstanding New

For production rights for *The Gene Pool*, please contact the author at 304-258-1223 or email christew@aol.com.

www.christistewartbrown.com

About the Author

Christi Stewart-Brown is an award-winning playwright who has had over 40 productions of her plays across the U.S., in Canada, and at the Edinburgh Fringe Festival in Scotland.

Stewart-Brown is a four-time Helen Hayes Award nominee and her plays include: *Morticians in Love*, which ran Off-Broadway in 1995 at the Perry Street Theatre, *The Gene Pool, Three More Sisters, Sweet Land of Liberty, Full of Grace, Steak!* (co-author), a country-western musical about cattle-rustling vegetarians, and *Do Not Use if Seal is Broken*, which was made into a film entitled *Loungers*.

Loungers, directed by Marc Forster *(Finding Neverland, Monster's Ball, The Kite Runner)*, was featured at the 1996 Slamdance Film Festival in Park City, Utah, where it won the Audience Award and placed second for the Jury Award.

She is also the author of the young adult novel *Kin*. She lives in West Virginia.

ACT ONE

Scene One

(AT RISE: Lights come up on an empty living room, perhaps even while the audience is still settling in. The opening bars of Doris Day's "Everybody Loves a Lover" blast. MIRA dances across the stage in ratty work clothes, carrying a varnish-covered paint brush. She exits.

She comes back on, half dressed, struggling into a nice shirt. She sings and bops her way back across the stage, picking up things, straightening the room, etc. She finds a lipstick and smears some on. She dances off.

She returns with a large cooking spoon and an oven mitt shaped like some sort of animal. She dims the lights, straightens more things, looks around to make sure everything is perfect, fluffs her hair. When the part of song plays in which Doris sings a round with herself, MIRA sings one part and puppets the oven mitt to 'sing' the other. 'They' share the spoon as a microphone. After the round is over, perhaps the oven mitt sings back up vocals as they head off. MIRA has exited by the time the final "Call me a Pollyanna..." is sung.

Sound of a door slamming, cutting the chorus off after the final "Pollyanna." Silence.

CLAIRE enters with a briefcase, blinks at the dimness, and turns the lights up brighter.)

CLAIRE: Honey, I'm home!

MIRA: *(off stage)* Be right out!

(CLAIRE sits at the table and takes some bills out of her briefcase. MIRA enters and dims the lights again. She tip-toes up behind CLAIRE and nuzzles her neck.)

CLAIRE: Hi sweetie.

MIRA: Hi there. How was your day?

CLAIRE: Oh, the usual. What'd you do today?

MIRA: Oh, this and that.

(CLAIRE continues to do paperwork. MIRA continues to nuzzle, then starts massaging CLAIRE'S back, then works her way down to her breasts.)

CLAIRE: Mira, what are you doing?

MIRA: Rubbing your breast.

CLAIRE: Why?

MIRA: Because it's nice.

CLAIRE: I'm trying to do bills.

MIRA: Can't you do them later?

CLAIRE: I'd like to do them now.

MIRA: You know what I'd like to do now?

CLAIRE: Mira...

(MIRA sighs, releases Claire's breast, and tries another tack.)

MIRA: I got your bookshelves finished.

CLAIRE: That was quick. Thanks, sweetie.

MIRA: The varnish isn't dry, so don't put anything on 'em yet.

CLAIRE: Okay.

MIRA: Oh, I just picked the last of the zucchini—I hope. Could you please take some into work with you? Give some to Sally or Blake or one of your patients' owners or something?

CLAIRE: Sweetie, nobody wants zucchini. Everybody plants it and it goes crazy and then they try to give it away. It's like some big fall ritual. Nobody actually eats that stuff.

MIRA: We eat it.

CLAIRE: No. You cook it, then Peter and I push it around our plates.

MIRA: You do?

CLAIRE: Yep.

MIRA: You just push it around?

CLAIRE: Mira... Could you just let me finish these—

MIRA: Yet the two of you encourage me to slave over a garden every spring...

CLAIRE: You like to garden.

MIRA: I like fresh vegetables. Do you two even like fresh vegetables?

CLAIRE: I like the broccoli, I like the carrots, the occasional beet. All I'm saying is that you can stop with the zucchini.

MIRA: Okay.

(The phone rings. MIRA picks it up.)

MIRA: Hello?...Hello?...*Helllll-Ooooh?*

(She hangs up.)

MIRA: I hate that.

(CLAIRE focuses more intently on her bills. MIRA puts on some soft music and dims the lights again. CLAIRE can't see what she's writing and puts down her pen, exasperated. She massages her neck with both hands. While she is doing this, MIRA sneaks up behind her and snaps a pair of pink furry handcuffs onto CLAIRE's wrists.)

CLAIRE: What the hell—?

MIRA: Now I've got you!

CLAIRE: What are you doing?

MIRA: *(straddling CLAIRE's lap)* How about a quick game of Master and Servant before Peter gets home?

CLAIRE: What?! Take these off me right now!

MIRA: Oh, c'mon Claire, I'm just trying to spice up your life.

CLAIRE: With handcuffs?

MIRA: Would you prefer silk ropes? They have some at the—

CLAIRE: No, I would not prefer ropes! What in the world have you been reading now?

MIRA: Nothing.

CLAIRE: Yes you have. Tell me.

MIRA: Nothing.

CLAIRE: Mira...

MIRA: Just a book.

CLAIRE: A book about...

MIRA: Just a book.

CLAIRE: Mira, take these off and tell me what the book is about.

MIRA: *(mumbling quietly, unlocking the cuffs)* Bed Death.

CLAIRE: Oh, God! You have got to stop reading those books!

MIRA: But we never make love anymore...

CLAIRE: We do too.

MIRA: When?

CLAIRE: You want an exact date?

MIRA: Yes.

CLAIRE: I can't give you an exact date.

MIRA: I can't either.

CLAIRE: I've been busy.

MIRA: We have Bed Death.

CLAIRE: We do not.

MIRA: They list the symptoms in my book.

CLAIRE: Work has been crazy, that's all.

MIRA: We have all the symptoms.

(PETER enters unnoticed. He's carrying a book bag.)

CLAIRE: I am not going to listen to this right now.

PETER: Hi Moms.

CLAIRE: Oh, hello dear.

PETER: What are you fighting about?

CLAIRE: We're not fighting, we're arguing. How was school?

PETER: Boring. What are you arguing about?

MIRA: Bed Death.

PETER: God, Mom! You can't talk about that stuff in front of your kid! Fuckin-A...

(He exits in disgust.)

MIRA: Well, he's certainly in a bad mood.

CLAIRE: He's been in a bad mood since he was thirteen.

MIRA: *(whispering)* I think it's because of his...you know...

CLAIRE: His what?

MIRA: *(pointing to her crotch)* You know...his...

CLAIRE: Oh...do you think?

MIRA: He can't leave it alone.

CLAIRE: What do you mean?

MIRA: He masturbates *all the time!*

CLAIRE: I don't wanna hear this, Mira...

MIRA: *All the time.*

CLAIRE: How do you know?

MIRA: I wash the sheets around here.

(CLAIRE makes a face of disgust. PETER returns, eating a snack, carrying a piece of paper, and scratching and rearranging his genitalia. MIRA and CLAIRE watch, fascinated.)

PETER: What's for dinner, Mom?

MIRA: Um...Coquille Saint Jacques.

PETER: Yuck. Why are you guys staring at me?

CLAIRE: Um...you're getting so tall.

PETER: Duh, Mom. Mom?

MIRA: Hm?

PETER: *(handing her the paper)* I don't get this question I missed on my Calculus quiz.

(MIRA studies the paper for a moment.)

MIRA: This isn't a *nonlinear* differential equation, it's linear.

PETER: But this function is raised to a power, that makes it nonlinear.

MIRA: But it's raised to the power of *one* . It has to be raised to a power other than one to make it nonlinear. That's the oldest trick question in the book.

PETER: That is so totally rude to trick people like that.

MIRA: It's how teachers get their kicks.

PETER: I guess. Mom?

CLAIRE: Yes, dear?

PETER: There's a guy at school who's selling his motorcycle really cheap—

CLAIRE: No.

PETER: Aw, c'mon, Mom! I can pay for most of it and you can pay for the rest for my birthday.

CLAIRE: I am not buying you a death machine for your birthday, there's no logic to that.

PETER: It's not a death machine.

(PETER looks to MIRA for help.)

MIRA: My brother had a motorcycle and he never got hurt.

CLAIRE: I don't want Peter riding one of those things. Buy yourself a car.

PETER: I don't want a car. I want a motorcycle.

CLAIRE: What's wrong with a car?

PETER: I don't want a car.

CLAIRE: Why not?

PETER: Cuz.

CLAIRE: I see.

PETER: I'm gonna be eighteen, you know. I don't even need your permission.

CLAIRE: But you do need a place to live. And you will not live here if you buy a motorcycle.

PETER: Maaaaaaa!

CLAIRE: You are not getting a motorcycle. End of discussion.

PETER: Fuckin-A!

(PETER stomps off. CLAIRE returns to her bills.)

MIRA: Honey, he'd be careful.

(CLAIRE stops writing and sighs.)

CLAIRE: I had to put Molly to sleep today.

MIRA: Molly Malone?

CLAIRE: Mm-hm.

MIRA: Oh, Pookie, I'm so sorry. Why didn't you say so?

CLAIRE: You didn't ask.

MIRA: Sh, sh. Poor darling.

CLAIRE: *(scribbling out a bill)* Y'know, the worst part about this profession is charging people for putting their pets to sleep. Billing for killing. It's so absurd.

MIRA: I know, sweetie. How's Mrs. Dalton?

CLAIRE: How do you think she is? She's upset!

MIRA: Sh, sh. Poor pumpkin.

(PETER enters eating something different.)

PETER: What's the matter?

MIRA: Your mother had to put Molly Malone to sleep today.

PETER: Who's Molly Malone?

MIRA: Old Mrs. Dalton's cat.

PETER: Bummer. Moms?

MIRA & CLAIRE: Yes, dear?

PETER: Can Paige come over tomorrow?

CLAIRE: Who's Paige?

PETER: My girlfriend.

MIRA: You have a girlfriend?

PETER: Yeah.

CLAIRE: You've never mentioned her.

PETER: She's new at school...we just sorta...you know...I mean she wasn't really my girlfriend until today.

CLAIRE: Why? What happened today?

PETER: I asked her to be my girlfriend.

CLAIRE: Oh.

PETER: She wants to meet you guys. Can she come over?

MIRA: She *may*. For dinner?

PETER: Yeah, I guess so.

MIRA: How exciting! I'll cook something extra-special.

PETER: Can't you just make something normal, like hamburgers, or macaroni and cheese?

MIRA: No.

PETER: Can you make something I can pronounce?

MIRA: Roasted chicken?

PETER: No zucchini.

MIRA: No zucchini.

CLAIRE: So tell us about Paige, dear.

PETER: *(he shrugs)* She's just a girl.

MIRA: Well, she must be a special girl, if our Peter likes her.

PETER: *(he shrugs)* Yeah. She's pretty cool. When's dinner?

MIRA: In about half an hour.

PETER: I'm gonna have a snack then.

MIRA: Just a little one.

PETER: Okay.

(PETER exits. MIRA runs to CLAIRE and hugs her from behind.)

MIRA: This is so exciting! Peter has a girlfriend.

CLAIRE: *(disentangling herself)* Uh-huh.

MIRA: You don't love me anymore.

CLAIRE: What? Look, I just killed Molly Malone, I don't love anyone right now, okay?

MIRA: Okay.

CLAIRE: I had a bad day.

MIRA: Well, I'm trying to cheer you up.

CLAIRE: Sweetie, furry handcuffs do not cheer me up. They're probably made out of somebody's cat I killed.

MIRA: I don't think so, honey—it's fake fur.

CLAIRE: I just...it seems like all I ever do anymore is put animals to sleep. I like the giving birth part of my job. I delivered a beautiful, healthy foal at the Robbins Place this morning, then I euthanized three cats and one dog this afternoon.

MIRA: Poor dear.

CLAIRE: And do you know why I got into this profession?

MIRA: The money?

CLAIRE: Because I love animals. And look around! Do you see a single pet? We don't have a single pet!

MIRA: Peter's allergic.

CLAIRE: You'd think we'd have a million pets. Strays. Cripples. Orphans. Sometimes I just want to come home to my own animals, not these...*transients* I deal with everyday—

MIRA: But Peter's allergic. Anyway, pets shed so much... And they smell.

CLAIRE: Not all of them.

MIRA: They drool. They whine. They meow. They eat the furniture. They want things, but they don't speak English. They poop...

CLAIRE: So do babies.

MIRA: I guess I've never really understood their purpose. I mean—"pets." What an odd name. "Pet." Some creature sits around waiting to be "pet." I'm going to pet my pet—

CLAIRE: This is what I'm saying!

MIRA: What?

CLAIRE: My career revolves around animals! You don't like them and Peter's allergic to them! What have I been doing for twenty years?!

MIRA: You're having a crisis, aren't you?

CLAIRE: I built this practice thinking my child would take it over! James Herriot's son took over *his* practice...

MIRA: But Peter's allergic.

CLAIRE: I know he's allergic—

MIRA: You think I'm saggy—

CLAIRE: So what am I supposed to do?—

MIRA: I do my Jane Fonda tape everyday—

CLAIRE: My son is allergic to my entire career!

MIRA: but I'm still saggy—

CLAIRE: I'll never be able to retire—

MIRA: Sometimes I have to rewind the tape—

CLAIRE: I'll have to go on killing cats until I'm ninety!

MIRA: because I'm getting slower...and saggier—

CLAIRE: I want my son to kill cats for me!—

MIRA: He can't do that. He's allergic—

CLAIRE: You are not saggy! And I know Peter is allergic to animals, okay?! I'm just trying to communicate that I'm a little bit depressed that our only offspring is not going to follow in my footsteps and that you have no connection whatsoever to my life's calling!

MIRA: I have a connection. I do.

CLAIRE: Phht! Every time I suggest going riding, you find some excuse.

MIRA: Horses are so sweaty...

CLAIRE: So are you when you walk around in the hot sun for a couple hours!

MIRA: I don't know what to say.

CLAIRE: I don't want you to say anything, I'm just venting! You always say you want me to talk more. WELL, I AM TALKING AND YOU ARE NOT LISTENING!

MIRA: If Peter wore a gas mask he might be able to kill cats...

CLAIRE: There's a little more to it than that! I do not just go to my office and KILL CATS!

(PETER enters eating something.)

PETER: Something's burning.

MIRA: Oh, no!

(MIRA runs off.)

CLAIRE: Peter?

PETER: Mom?

CLAIRE: Do you want to be a vet?

PETER: I don't wanna kill cats...

CLAIRE: Because we can get you allergy shots...

PETER: Fuckin-A, Mom. I don't wanna kill cats. I like cats.

CLAIRE: I also help give birth to animals, I make sick animals well. I encourage life, I don't just put an end to it.

PETER: Yeah, but...I'm allergic...

CLAIRE: There are shots...

PETER: I'm afraid of needles...

CLAIRE: Okay, fine. What *do* you want to be, Peter? You're going to college next year...somewhere. What do you want to study?

PETER: I dunno. That's so far away.

CLAIRE: It's not far away. It's next year.

PETER: I can't think that far ahead.

CLAIRE: What *do* you think about, Peter?

PETER: Sex.

CLAIRE: Is that all?

PETER: Pretty much.

CLAIRE: Have you...um...ever...*had* ...sex?

PETER: No. I'm a virgin. Can you believe that? I'm almost eighteen!

CLAIRE: Uh-huh. Speaking of which, what do you want to do on your birthday? Shall we go out to dinner?

PETER: Nah. I'm gonna hang with Paige.

CLAIRE: Oh.

PETER: I wanna lose my virginity on my birthday and Paige said she'd help me.

CLAIRE: Help you?

PETER: You know what I mean.

CLAIRE: Uh-huh. And is Paige the right girl?

PETER: Right girl? She's a girl. I like her a lot. She likes me a lot. We want to have sex .

CLAIRE: Well, there you go.

(MIRA enters carrying a potholder.)

MIRA: It was just the rice. I had to start a new batch, so it'll take another half hour. You'd better have a snack, Peter.

PETER: Okay.

(He starts to exit.)

CLAIRE: Wait a second, Peter. Tell your mother what you want to do for your birthday.

MIRA: Dinner at Hamburger Heaven? Friday the Thirteenth, Part 47?

PETER: I wanna lose my virginity.

MIRA: With Paige?

PETER: Yeah.

MIRA: Wow.

PETER: Is that okay?

MIRA: Shoot yeah. Can't think of anything I would've rather done when I was eighteen. Except I was sixteen. Eighteen is a little late for a guy, isn't it?

PETER: That is so sexist, Mom! Eighteen is late for everyone these days!

MIRA: Yeah, I guess so.

PETER: *(starts to exit, then stops)* Oh, yeah. Can one of you guys buy me some condoms?

CLAIRE: Why can't you buy your own?

PETER: Fuckin-A, Mom. That would be so embarrassing!

CLAIRE: Well, if you're old enough to have sex—

MIRA: Oh, I'll get some at the Safeway.

CLAIRE: Mira...

MIRA: He's embarrassed. But if he's gonna ride, he has to wear a helmet.

PETER: Maaaaa!

(PETER exits.)

CLAIRE: So when he's away at college, you'll fed-ex him condoms?

MIRA: Sure.

CLAIRE: You can't be responsible for your son's sex life, Mira.

MIRA: Maybe I'm just glad someone's getting it around here.

CLAIRE: Jesus, Mira. Look, sweetie, I've just been busy and distracted and neglectful and I'm sorry. How about we go dancing Friday? We'll go to the country-western place and you can twirl me 'round the dance floor.

MIRA: Really?

CLAIRE: Really. Dinner and dancing.

MIRA: You're on! Give us a kiss and I'll go back to my kitchen.

(CLAIRE gives MIRA a kiss. MIRA jumps up, energized. She charges off to the kitchen, clutching her pot holder.)

BLACKOUT

Scene Two

(The next evening.

Music plays: Doris Day's "Que Sera, Sera". The stage is lit primarily by candles. CLAIRE enters carrying a briefcase. Her right hand is bandaged. She is bewildered by the darkness and bumps into things, groping for the light switch.)

CLAIRE: Honey, I'm home! Why are the lights off? Hello?

(She finds the switch and turns on the lights. The phone rings. CLAIRE picks it up. Throughout the conversation, she continually glances around trying to figure out where Mira is.)

CLAIRE: Hello? *(her voice drops to a whisper)* You have to stop calling me...No.... just call Blake if one of the horses is sick...No...Look, I'm sorry...Because I just can't anymore, we've gone through this...Well, I'm sorry, but there's nothing I can do...I have to go...No, absolutely not... Don't cry...I'm hanging up, now, okay?...I'm sorry...

(CLAIRE hangs up the phone. She is shaky and upset.)

CLAIRE: Mira?

She heads for the table, to put her briefcase down. The lights go off. She goes to the switch and turns them on and heads back toward the table...they go off again. MIRA enters in the candlelight. She creeps up behind CLAIRE and hugs her. CLAIRE screams. MIRA screams.

CLAIRE: Good God!

(CLAIRE turns the lights on. MIRA is wearing Saran Wrap. Underneath the Saran Wrap, she is wearing a bra and panties. She strikes a "sexy" pose when the lights come on.)

MIRA: Hi, honey.

CLAIRE: Hi. Where were you—? My God, what are you wearing?

MIRA: Saran Wrap.

CLAIRE: Have you been reading "The Total Woman" or something?

MIRA: Maybe.

CLAIRE: That book is hopelessly out of date, Mira.

MIRA: I thought she had some very good ideas...

CLAIRE: You're not supposed to wear anything underneath.

MIRA: What?

CLAIRE: You're wearing underwear.

MIRA: They're sexy underwear.

CLAIRE: I think the idea is to...never mind.

MIRA: Does it turn you on?

CLAIRE: No, Mira, it does not "turn me on." You've got to stop reading those books.

MIRA: *(slinking up and putting her arms around CLAIRE)* If I took off the underwear would it turn you on?

CLAIRE: No.

MIRA: Well, can you give me some idea of what would?

CLAIRE: I said I'd take you dancing.

MIRA: Fine. But I also want some spontaneity. You can't just take me out dancing when you feel guilty about neglecting me.

CLAIRE: You're right. Mira, I need to talk to you... I don't know how to say this—

(PETER enters. He stares at MIRA.)

PETER: Holy shit, Mom! Have you been reading "The Total Woman" or something?

CLAIRE: How do you know about that?

PETER: I had to read it in my Women's Studies class. Fuckin-A, Mom! That book is so out of date.

MIRA: Well, I liked it.

PETER: Mom, tell her to change. Paige is coming over. She can't dress like that in front of Paige!

CLAIRE: Mira...

MIRA: I'm going. I'm changing.

(MIRA exits in a huff.)

PETER: *(yelling off toward MIRA)* And you're not supposed to wear underwear! *(to himself)* I'm hungry.

(PETER exits to get a snack. CLAIRE sighs and sits at the table with her briefcase. She begins taking papers out. She rubs her injured hand and checks the bandage. The doorbell rings. CLAIRE waits for Peter to get it. The doorbell rings again.)

PETER: *(off stage)* Mom! Someone's at the door!

CLAIRE: She's your girlfriend, Peter. Let her in and introduce her to us properly.

PETER: *(off stage)* Fuckin-A.

(After a moment, PETER enters, followed by PAIGE. PAIGE carries a motorcycle helmet. CLAIRE stands and smiles.)

PETER: Hey dude.

PAIGE: Hey.

PETER: Mom, this is Paige.

PAIGE: Hi.

CLAIRE: Nice to meet you, Paige.

(CLAIRE starts to shake hands, then remembers the injury and just sort of waves at her.)

PETER: What happened to your hand, Mom?

CLAIRE: Dog bite.

PAIGE: Oooo, bummer. You're a vet, right?

CLAIRE: That's right.

PAIGE: I'm thinking about becoming a vet.

CLAIRE: Really?

PETER: Why do you wanna do that? Dogs'll bite you.

(MIRA enters dressed normally. Stuck to the bottom of her shoe is a long piece of Saran Wrap, which CLAIRE will spend the better part of the scene trying to surreptitiously remove.)

MIRA: Hello, hello! You must be Paige.

PETER: Mom, this is Paige.

MIRA: How lovely to meet you.

PAIGE: Hi.

MIRA: Shall we sit? Have you offered Paige something to drink, dear?

PETER: You want something to drink?

PAIGE: Coke?

PETER: Okay. Be right back. Uh...anyone else?

MIRA: I'm fine, thanks.

CLAIRE: No, thanks.

PETER exits.

MIRA: What happened to your hand, Claire?

CLAIRE: Dog bite.

MIRA: Pets! *(to PAIGE)* Sit, sit, sit! Make yourself at home.

PAIGE: Thanks.

MIRA: So...you're Peter's girlfriend.

PAIGE: Yes ma'am.

MIRA: She's so polite! I love that.

(PAIGE looks around, unsure where to put her helmet.)

PAIGE: Mrs. Gray...I mean... I'm sorry...I never asked Peter what your last names were.

MIRA: You were right. Gray. We're all Gray here!

PAIGE: That's a coincidence.

CLAIRE: Well, we weren't born with the name Gray.

MIRA: No, no. Ironically, my maiden name is *Black* and hers is *White*, isn't that funny? So when we got together, we met in the middle.

PAIGE: Cool.

MIRA: Get it? Black and White together make—

CLAIRE: She gets it, dear.

PAIGE: Yes ma'am.

CLAIRE: I notice you have a motorcycle helmet there.

PAIGE: I was gonna ask where to put it...

CLAIRE: Anywhere's fine.

(PAIGE places it on the coffee table, MIRA picks it up and puts it on the floor under the coffee table.)

PAIGE: Sorry.

MIRA: No, no. That's a nice helmet.

CLAIRE: So...you ride a motorcycle...

PAIGE: Yes, ma'am.

MIRA: How do your parents feel about you riding a motorcycle?

PAIGE: Well, my mom rides a Harley...

MIRA: Wow. Where're you from?

PAIGE: South Dakota. Near Rapid City.

MIRA: Great place to ride. The Black Hills...we were there years ago.

PAIGE: Yeah, that's a great ride through there.

(PETER enters with two cokes. They watch him sit. Silence.)

MIRA: So...tell us what you like about our Peter.

PETER: Fuckin-A, Mom...

PAIGE: Umm...he's cute.

CLAIRE: Is he?

MIRA: Claire! He's gorgeous!

PETER: I am not "cute."

MIRA: Of course you are.

PETER: Mom...

(Pause. Nobody knows what to talk about. PAIGE gropes for a topic.)

PAIGE: So...um...which one of you is Peter's real mother?

(Total, utter, complete, dead silence. MIRA fidgets with the helmet with her feet. PETER sticks a finger in his coke and stirs the ice. CLAIRE stares at PAIGE.)

PAIGE: Oh, God. Sorry. Wrong question.

CLAIRE: We are *both* Peter's mothers.

PAIGE: I'm sorry.

CLAIRE: It's okay.

PAIGE: No, I...um...

(More silence. MIRA tries to help.)

MIRA: Say, Peter, did we ever tell you the story of how you got your name?

PETER: Grandpa's name is Peter.

MIRA: Oh my God, you're right! But that's not how you got your name.

CLAIRE: Mira...

PETER: It isn't?

MIRA: This is a cute story, Paige. You'll like it.

CLAIRE: Oh, Mira...

MIRA: When we were pregnant, we naturally thought we'd have a girl. I mean...you know... *(gesturing as if to say that two females would naturally have another)* Anyway, we had all these girls names picked out...and then in the delivery room the doctor says "It's a boy!" and we just stared at him. We couldn't believe it was a boy. And I said to Claire, "It's got a peter!" And so—

PETER: That is not true!

MIRA: It is.

PETER: Fuckin-A, Mom! You named me after my... my—?

MIRA: Well...in a way...no, not really...

PETER: I don't believe this! Nice embarrassment job in front of Paige, guys. Let's go. We're going to my room to listen to music. Call when dinner's ready.

MIRA: Okay.

(PETER and PAIGE start to exit.)

CLAIRE: Sweetheart?

PETER: Yeah?

CLAIRE: It's a beautiful name. It's a Saint's name.

PETER: Whatever.

(PETER and PAIGE exit.)

CLAIRE: You shouldn't have told that story. And you have Saran Wrap stuck to your shoe.

MIRA: I shouldn't? I do?

(MIRA pulls the Saran Wrap off of her shoe and plays with it.)

CLAIRE: You embarrassed him.

MIRA: I didn't mean to.

CLAIRE: People take their names seriously.

MIRA: I suppose...

CLAIRE: We named him after his penis—and while it is a lovely name—I don't think he appreciates that.

MIRA: I'll apologize.

CLAIRE: After Paige leaves...

MIRA: After Paige leaves.

(PETER enters the living room. His clothes and hair are a bit disheveled.)

PETER: Mom? Did you get the...the 'you knows'?

MIRA: The condoms?

PETER: Yeah.

MIRA: They're for your birthday.

PETER: Yeah, but...

MIRA: Dinner's almost ready. You don't have time, and this is something I really want to stress. You *have to take the time.* When you masturbate, it may take you five minutes—

PETER: Fuckin-A, Mom!

MIRA: But when you're with a girl, you need to make sure she's satisfied. And that takes more than five minutes.

PETER: Okay.

MIRA: Are you listening?

PETER: Yeah.

MIRA: I mean are you really listening?

PETER: Yes!

MIRA: You don't want to be a bad lover, do you?

PETER: Mom!

MIRA: You get the condoms on your birthday.

PETER: Okay! Can we go for a ride on Paige's bike then?

MIRA: Dinner'll be ready soon.

PETER: Just a quick ride. I just gotta do *something*—know what I mean?

MIRA: Uh-huh. Okay, a quick ride.

CLAIRE: Does she have an extra helmet?

PETER: Yes, Mother.

(PETER grabs the helmet from under the coffee table and exits.)

MIRA: Should I have given them to him?

CLAIRE: They're a birthday present.

MIRA: Right.

CLAIRE: Right.

MIRA: Come help me get dinner on.

CLAIRE: I need a drink.

MIRA: *(flicking the saran wrap at her playfully as they exit)* Would it loosen you up?

CLAIRE: Mira, please...

MIRA: It was just a joke, Claire. Lighten up.

(They exit.

Lights up on the motorcycle. PETER and PAIGE are standing by the bike. PAIGE unlocks a second helmet and hands it to PETER.)

PAIGE: I'm sorry I fucked up in there. I shouldn't have asked that.

PETER: No biggie.

PAIGE: But I'm totally curious. I mean like which one is your mother?

PETER: They both are.

PAIGE: Yeah, yeah. But which one gave *birth* to you?

PETER: Both.

PAIGE: That's not possible.

PETER: It's complicated.

PAIGE: *(getting on the bike)* I'm sorry. There I go again. Total diarrhea of the mouth.

PETER: It's okay.

PAIGE: Who's your father?

PETER: I don't have a father.

PAIGE: Dude...*that* is not possible.

PETER: Well, I don't know who it is.

PAIGE: Aren't you curious?

PETER: No.

(PAIGE cranks the engine and revs it. They have to yell over the noise. PETER climbs on behind PAIGE and wraps his arms around her waist. PAIGE "takes off" and they both jolt slightly backward. Throughout this next they lean around curves in unison, etc.)

PAIGE: What about your medical history? You should have your medical history.

PETER: I'm not sick.

PAIGE: For the future. It's always good to know that sort of stuff just in case.

PETER: Never thought about it.

PAIGE: God, I'd be obsessed.

(PETER shrugs.)

PAIGE: What if you look like him? You don't really look like your Moms.

PETER: I look like me.

PAIGE: Was it a guy they knew?

PETER: I don't think so. It was all artificial insemination and stuff like that. I was conceived in a lab.

PAIGE: Just an anonymous sperm donor?

PETER: I guess so.

PAIGE: What if your dad is a Nobel Prize winner or something?

PETER: That'd be cool. But what if he's serial killer or something?

PAIGE: Don't even joke about that shit. God, this is driving me crazy. It's like a big mystery!

PETER: Are we still gonna have sex on my birthday?

PAIGE: Sure. Are you gonna get the...?

PETER: My mom has 'em.

PAIGE: You told your mom?

PETER: Sure.

PAIGE: Which one?

PETER: Both.

PAIGE: God, I'm so embarrassed.

PETER: They're cool.

PAIGE: I can't eat dinner with them. I'm mortified.

PETER: Don't be.

PAIGE: I feel like such a slut.

PETER: That is so—

PAIGE: Sexist, I know. Okay. Okay, if you don't feel like a slut, I don't. I'm fine. Really.

PETER: Okay.

PAIGE: Okay.

(PAIGE stops at a stop sign. They jolt a bit forward, put their legs down on the ground to balance the bike, look both ways, etc.)

PETER: How long does it take?

PAIGE: What?

PETER: Sex. How long does it take for girls?

PAIGE: What do you mean?

PETER: My mom said it takes longer for girls...

PAIGE: Okay, now I'm mortified.

PAIGE peels out. PETER is thrown backwards and almost loses his seat. He grabs onto PAIGE and holds her tighter.

BLACKOUT.

Scene Three

Evening. The living room is dark. CLAIRE enters with her briefcase.

CLAIRE: Honey, I'm— *(She sees the darkness again. She sighs. She stands, not even attempting to turn the lights on.)* Mira, don't do this to me. I had a terrible day. There was an accident. One of those double-decker-horse-carrying-truck-things overturned on the highway.

There were horses everywhere. Horses missing legs...heads...tails. I had to euthanize fifteen of them. Four died on their own. One horse lived. One damn horse out of twenty. And the asshole driving the truck was mad because his truck was totaled! Mira?

Are you listening to me? I mean there's death and destruction everywhere and he's upset about his goddamned truck! Those poor horses are dead and they didn't understand what was happening to them. They don't understand traffic. They just...they just got on the truck because some other asshole told them to. Mira?

(She stumbles to the couch, sits, puts her head in her bandaged hand, and sobs. After a moment, PETER enters carrying a motorcycle helmet. He turns on the lights. CLAIRE jumps.)

PETER: Hey, Mom.

CLAIRE: Oh, hello, dear.

PETER: Why're you sitting in the dark?

CLAIRE: I thought...well, I thought your mom had them off on purpose to be romantic and—

PETER: I don't wanna hear that stuff—

CLAIRE: No, I mean... MIRA!? Maybe she's not even home.

(PETER picks up a note from the table and reads.)

PETER: "Be back soon, Pardner. Went to rustle up some new duds." She's not here, Mom.

CLAIRE: Guess not. *(noticing the helmet)* What's that?

PETER: A helmet.

CLAIRE: A motorcycle helmet.

PETER: Paige didn't feel like driving me home, so she gave me the bike.

CLAIRE: I thought you were having dinner with Paige and her family.

PETER: I did. They eat like right when you walk through the door. No conversation, no "how was your day, honey?" It's like dinner is *there*. Eat it now or *starve*. So I ate it. And then there was nothing to do. I'm not allowed to go to her room and I didn't wanna watch TV with her family, so I came home.

CLAIRE: Why can't you go to her room?

PETER: I dunno. Guess they figure something might happen, which it might.

CLAIRE: So you took the motorcycle...

PETER: It's such a rush, Mom! Have you ever been on one?

CLAIRE: No.

PETER: God, it's like the wind is right there in your face and you totally notice what color the leaves are, and how buildings are built, and drops of water on the pavement, and everything around you—

CLAIRE: And the other people in traffic?

PETER: Don't be such a drag! Of course I notice the traffic.

CLAIRE: Good.

PETER: Man, you look like you killed a hundred cats today.

CLAIRE: Something like that.

PETER: You need a ride.

CLAIRE: A ride where?

PETER: On the bike. C'mon, I'm gonna take you for a ride!

(PETER hands the helmet to CLAIRE. She fidgets with it.)

PETER: C'mon, Mom! You'll love it. You'll forget all about the cats.

CLAIRE: Horses.

PETER: Whatever. Put it on.

(CLAIRE hesitates, then puts the helmet on.)

PETER: How's it feel?

CLAIRE: Scary.

PETER: C'mon, let's go.

CLAIRE: What about your head?

PETER: There's an extra helmet on the bike.

CLAIRE: I don't know...

PETER: *(heading out)* Come on, Maaaa!

(CLAIRE follows PETER off. They reappear by the motorcycle and PETER unlocks the second helmet.)

CLAIRE: No, wait. What if we crash and there's arms and legs and tails everywhere?

PETER: God, Mom. You ride horses all the time. You could get thrown from a horse and break your neck!

CLAIRE: But horses just seem so much more reasonable than motorcycles. You can talk to them and pet them and all that.

PETER: They still do whatever they want. You can control a bike easier than a horse.

CLAIRE: But I can relate to horses. I can't relate to machines. I can't even work the microwave unless you help me.

PETER: Maaa!

CLAIRE: I'm not a modern woman, Peter.

PETER: *Carpe diem*, dude. That's Latin for—

CLAIRE: I know.

PETER: C'mon, Ma. I'll go slow. I promise.

CLAIRE: Very slow.

(PETER cranks the bike up and revs the engine.)

PETER: Get on.

(CLAIRE climbs on behind PETER. She holds onto him very tightly. PETER gasps for air.)

PETER: I can't breathe, Ma!

CLAIRE: Sorry.

PETER: Okay, here we go!

(CLAIRE lets out a shriek as they pull out. She buries her head in PETER's shoulder and won't look at the road. They lean around a few curves and CLAIRE gradually looks around her. She breathes deeply and smiles. PETER turns around and smiles at her, she immediately points for him to look at the road, not her. She sits up straighter and loosens her grip on PETER. Suddenly, she lets go of PETER and puts her hands straight up in the air and yells, "Wheeee." She loses her nerve and grabs PETER again. They both laugh.

Lights fade on the motorcycle and come up in the living room. MIRA enters wearing a country-western outfit, and carrying a shopping bag. She pulls a cowboy hat out of the bag and plunks it on her head.)

MIRA: Claire? Sorry I'm late! Let's go show them cowpokes how to dance! Claire?

(MIRA wanders off stage, then back on, calling for Claire. She finds her own note, then looks around for a reciprocal one. She goes to the telephone and dials.)

MIRA: Sally? Hey, it's Mira. Sorry to call you at home. I'm just wondering if Claire had an emergency or something. We were supposed to—oh, dear. How awful. So they're still there. Oh. What time did she head home then? I see. Well, maybe she went for a beer with Blake after all that. I sure would. Thanks anyway, Sally. Say hey to Tim for me...Okay. Bye.

(MIRA hangs up the phone, then picks it up and dials another number.)

MIRA: Oh, hi Blake...you're home...It's Mira. Sally told me about the accident, so I thought maybe you went out for beer— Oh. Okay. Say hey to Max for me...Okay. Bye.

(MIRA hangs up the phone, then picks it up and dials another number.)

MIRA: Hey, it's me...No, nothing's wrong... No, Peter's fine. I'm just calling to say hey. Nothing's wrong, Mom....Yeah.....a little...uh-huh...she's a lot like Daddy...Yeah, I tried that...no, nothing....Really? *(she laughs)* Daddy? I can't imagine... Okay...well, I'd better go. We're supposed to go dancing tonight. Say hey to Daddy for me....I know, Mother. I meant next time you visit his grave... Okay, I will...love you, too.

(MIRA hangs up and wanders around aimlessly for a bit. She goes to the stereo and puts on some country-western music. She sings along with the music and dances around a bit by herself. Suddenly, she sits down and starts crying.

Lights come up behind her on the motorcycle. CLAIRE is driving. She applies the brakes, and the bike wobbles a little bit.)

CLAIRE: Whoa, girl.

(PETER puts his feet down to steady the bike, then reaches around and switches off the engine. CLAIRE pats the bike like it's a horse, then pulls her helmet off, grinning.)

CLAIRE: I did it!

PETER: You were awesome, Mom.

CLAIRE: It did what I told it to!

(PETER laughs. They head inside, chattering. MIRA hears them coming and wipes her nose on her sleeve.)

CLAIRE: *(off stage)* That was really amazing! What a rush! Is that what it's called?

(PETER and CLAIRE enter the living room.)

PETER: See? I told you— *(he spots MIRA)* Hi Mom!

CLAIRE: Mira, guess what? I rode on Paige's motorcycle and then Peter taught me how to drive it and I went around the block all by myself and—

MIRA: Peter, I'd like you to go to your room.

PETER: Is Mom in trouble?

MIRA: She is.

CLAIRE: *(looking at her watch, suddenly remembering their date)* Oh, God, I'm so sorry, I—

PETER: Well, it's probably my fault, whatever it is, 'cause I—

MIRA: GO!

PETER: I'm totally gone.

(PETER hustles off.)

CLAIRE: Oh, sweetie, I'm so sorry. It's not that late, let's go now.

MIRA: Forget it. That's not the point.

CLAIRE: I'm sorry, I just had a bad day and Peter—

MIRA: You always have a bad day!

CLAIRE: No, I mean a *really* bad day. There was this big accident with a horse trailer—

MIRA: I don't care if every horse in the county keeled over dead today!

CLAIRE: Don't say that.

MIRA: *(hurling her cowboy hat at CLAIRE)* WE HAD A DATE!

CLAIRE: I said I'm sorry!! Look, I came home, I felt lousy, and I went for a ride with Peter. You weren't even home!

MIRA: I left you a goddamned note! You could've at least done me the same courtesy! But no! You're as thoughtless as your son! Both of you just go off and leave me whenever you feel like it!

CLAIRE: What's Peter got to do with this?

MIRA: I spend all day at home, trying to make it a nice place for you two ingrates. I clean, I cook, I empty the trash, I mow the lawn, I plant the garden, and you both take it for granted that I'll just be here to listen to your problems when you get home.

CLAIRE: I think you're having a mid-life crisis, Mira—

MIRA: But nobody wants to listen to my problems! No one asks if *I've* had a bad day and need some help feeling better!

CLAIRE: Or pre-empty nest syndrome or something—

MIRA: I'm your doormat! Your faithful dog, who gets a pat on the head now and then by its two thoughtless owners!

CLAIRE: Well, if it's so terrible for you, Mira, why don't you get out of the house more? Join a club! Take a class! Have an affair! Get a job! Get a *life*, for Christ's sake!

(MIRA is stunned.)

MIRA: How *dare* you! YOU are my life! PETER is my life!

CLAIRE: I'm sorry—

MIRA: And you're both wandering away from me. God! I'm gonna be totally alone!

CLAIRE: I'm sorry, sweetie, I shouldn't have—

MIRA: Wait a second. Did you just tell me to have an affair?

CLAIRE: Well, I didn't mean—

MIRA: Why did you say that?

CLAIRE: It's just something you say...like I didn't really mean "get a life"...I was just saying...

MIRA: What an odd thing to say to me. I would never think of saying something like that.

CLAIRE: It was just a—

MIRA: And I would never think of...

(MIRA narrows her eyes and stares at CLAIRE for a long time. This makes CLAIRE very uncomfortable. MIRA looks a little dizzy. She sits.)

MIRA: When?

CLAIRE: It's over, Mira

MIRA: When, goddammit?!

CLAIRE: It didn't mean anything...

MIRA: Tell me *when!!!*

CLAIRE: It was stupid, it was just—

MIRA: Are we talking recent here?!

CLAIRE: Mira...

MIRA: It's over since *when*?!

CLAIRE: Last week.

MIRA: Last week? Last *week?!!!*

CLAIRE: It didn't mean anything.

MIRA: Were you planning to tell me about this?

CLAIRE: Yes. I was going to...I tried...

MIRA: Who was she?

CLAIRE: I can't tell you that.

MIRA: Oh. Yes, of course. By all means, protect *her*. It's okay if I go to the grocery store or the video store or the hardware store and run into her and smile like a fool. That's okay. Just make sure to protect *her.*

CLAIRE: You don't know her.

MIRA: Oh, good. Now I feel better. A complete stranger has made a fool of me. God, you probably gave her some of my zucchini! Did you give her some of my zucchini?

CLAIRE: Of course not.

MIRA: Wow. You actually...? *(she sits silently for a moment)* With someone else...? You actually...I can't even say it. This is really beyond my comprehension. I don't know what to say. I don't even know where to begin...

CLAIRE: It didn't mean anything.

MIRA: Stop saying that! It devalues whoever it was. And you. I don't think I really want to know you're that shallow.

CLAIRE: I think I was just felt like I needed—

MIRA: You needed something and it couldn't come from me.

CLAIRE: No.

MIRA: Yes.

CLAIRE: Maybe. I don't know. I can explain—

MIRA: You can?! You mean there's actually a valid explanation for this behavior?

CLAIRE: I just meant—

MIRA: Well, as long as you have a good explanation, Claire, I'm sure everything'll be just fine and dandy!

CLAIRE: I'm only trying to—

MIRA: Shut up, Claire! Right now I'm just trying to grasp this. How about if I just ask you for details when I'm ready to hear them?

CLAIRE: Okay.

MIRA: I need to think.

CLAIRE: Okay.

(MIRA stands. She's a bit wobbly.)

MIRA: In the meantime, I think you're probably right. I should go out and get myself a life.

CLAIRE: Mira, I didn't mean that—

MIRA: Maybe I need more than just the two of you. Obviously, you need more than just the two of us...

CLAIRE: I'm so sorry.

MIRA: Me too, Claire. Maybe I'll get a job.

CLAIRE: I don't want you to get a job.

MIRA: You just told me to get a job, among other things...

CLAIRE: I was angry. I didn't mean it.

MIRA: I think it's a good idea.

CLAIRE: Well, I don't.

MIRA: *(glaring at her)* Well, too bad.

(MIRA goes to the table and picks up the newspaper. She rifles through the it until she finds the classified section.)

CLAIRE: Mira, don't do this just because you're mad at me.

MIRA: I'm not. I've been thinking about it anyway. I need to have something to do when Peter leaves home. I don't think either of you realize how hard that's going to be for me. Typical of you both. I bet she was young. Was she young?

CLAIRE: *(ignoring the question)* What kind of job are you going to get? What can you do?

MIRA: I'm a math whiz.

CLAIRE: I know, but you can't just look in the want-ads under "Math Whiz". You haven't been in the job market for— Have you ever been in the job market?

MIRA: Nope. Daddy supported me in college, then you supported me. But I *want* a job. I hear that people who are unemployed don't really *want* jobs. I *want* a job, therefore, I will get one. The power of positive thinking. Was she a blonde? At least tell me she wasn't a blonde.

CLAIRE: She wasn't a blonde.

(MIRA abruptly tucks the newspaper and starts to exit.)

MIRA: Good. I'm gonna go read these in bed. You'll be sleeping out here, of course.

CLAIRE: No, wait, Mira. Stay and talk to me. Don't go to bed angry.

MIRA: Don't go to bed angry?! You know what, Claire? If I wait until I'm not angry about this to go to bed, I won't get any sleep for months! Did she have one of those Rubenesque figures?

CLAIRE: Oh, for God's sake. If you want to talk, let's talk. Don't just keep throwing out these—

MIRA: Or maybe she one of those "horsey women" who go everywhere dressed like they're fox hunting.

(CLAIRE looks away. MIRA notices and drops into a chair.)

MIRA: Oh, my God. I'm right, aren't I?

(CLAIRE nods.)

MIRA: I thought you hated those clothes.

CLAIRE: It wasn't about clothes—

MIRA: Of course not. She probably wasn't even wearing clothes most of time. It was about horses.

CLAIRE: Not just horses. Animals in general. I was attracted to her love of animals. We just had so much in common...

(MIRA clamps her hands over her ears and closes her eyes.)

MIRA: No more.

CLAIRE: And I felt like I could talk to her about things I can't talk to you about.

MIRA: *That's enough!*

CLAIRE: I need to talk to you about this.

MIRA: I don't care what you need! You should have told me about your needs before you went off and found someone else to take care of them! This is about *my* needs now. And right now I need to get away from you!

(MIRA stomps off, clutching her newspaper. After a moment, PETER enters.)

PETER: Hi Mom. Where's Mom?

CLAIRE: She's reading want ads, looking for a job.

PETER: Do we need money?

CLAIRE: She just wants a job.

PETER: Is she having a mid-life crisis?

CLAIRE: I think she just wants to get out more.

PETER: Oh.

(The phone rings. PETER picks it up.)

PETER: Hello?....HELLO?....Get a life!

(He slams the phone down.)

CLAIRE: No one there?

PETER: I hate that. What's for dinner?

CLAIRE: You already had dinner at Paige's.

PETER: I'm hungry again, so I'll have some of whatever you guys are having.

CLAIRE: Your Mom didn't cook anything.

PETER: What are you gonna eat?

CLAIRE: I'm not hungry.

PETER: Fuckin-A... What am I supposed to eat?

CLAIRE: Look, sweetie, I'm sorry there's no extra dinner for you. I'd make you something, but I don't know how to cook. I'm a terrible Mom, I know—

PETER: It's not your job, it's Mom's job.

CLAIRE: Well, that may have to change. Put something in the microwave, okay?

PETER: I guess.

(MIRA enters, dumps a pillow and blanket on the floor, then exits.)

PETER: You sleeping out here tonight?

CLAIRE: Yeah.

PETER: Just 'cause you rode a motorcycle?

CLAIRE: It's complicated. Don't worry about it.

PETER: Okay. Mom?

CLAIRE: Yes, dear?

PETER: Who's my father?

CLAIRE: Oh, God. Can we talk about this later?

PETER: Yeah, sure.

CLAIRE: It's a long story. Your Mom should be here for it, but now is not the time. Okay?

PETER: Okay.

CLAIRE: Okay. I'm gonna turn in now. It's been a hard day.

PETER: *(looking for reassurance)* The horses, huh?

CLAIRE: Yeah. It was pretty yucky. 'Night, sweetie. Love you.

PETER: Love you back.

(PETER scratches and adjusts his genitalia. He is only vaguely satisfied by CLAIRE's answer.)

PETER: *(to himself)* Fuckin-A.

(PETER shuffles off. CLAIRE tips over and curls up on the couch.)

BLACKOUT

End of Act One.

ACT TWO

Scene One

(AT RISE: The next evening. CLAIRE sits doing paperwork at the table. PETER watches her as he eats a snack. The house already looks messier.)

PETER: How much do you charge to kill a cat?

CLAIRE: Twenty-five dollars.

PETER: Fuckin-A. You could tie a rock around its neck and throw it in the river for free!

CLAIRE: Don't talk like that.

PETER: How much do you charge to kill a dog?

CLAIRE: Same.

PETER: A horse?

CLAIRE: Fifty dollars.

PETER: That seems reasonable. Do you shoot 'em or stick 'em?

CLAIRE: Stick 'em...unless it's an emergency. I had to shoot a horse at the accident the other day.

PETER: Mom with a gun! Way cool! Um...how much do you charge to help give birth to a baby horse?

CLAIRE: A *foal*. Are you bored?

PETER: I'm hungry. Fuckin-A. For eighteen years there's always been food waiting for me, or at least in the oven cooking for me. Suddenly, there's no food. What's for dinner?

CLAIRE: Maybe we can order out.

PETER: I want a burger.

CLAIRE: Nobody delivers burgers, sweetie. Why don't you have a snack?

(PETER sighs and exits. MIRA enters. She is quite chuffed with herself.)

MIRA: Hello!

CLAIRE: Hi.

MIRA: Oh. Hi. Where's Peter?

CLAIRE: Getting a snack. How'd it go today?

MIRA: Fine. PETER!!!

(PETER enters eating a snack.)

PETER: Hey Mom.

MIRA: I have an announcement.

CLAIRE: You got a job.

MIRA: Of course I got a job. I start day after tomorrow, and let this be a lesson to you, Peter. Your mother got a job because she *wanted* one.

PETER: Okay.

CLAIRE: What kind of job is it?

MIRA: I'm working down at Tom's Tow Lot.

PETER: What's that?

MIRA: That's where they take cars that have been towed. When people come to get their cars, they have to ask me for their cars and they have to give me money to get their cars back. I have this adorable little Airstream trailer all to myself and I'll be meeting people from all walks of life—I mean anyone can get their car towed, it crosses all socioeconomic boundaries.

CLAIRE: I thought you wanted to use your math, sweetie.

MIRA: Well, that's the great part. I do get to use my math. Tom and I talked for a while about how mad people get at him when all he's doing is towing cars that the police tell him to tow. So I came up with this really neat sliding scale system for the customers and Tom agreed to try it out, but to use it you have to be able add in your head really fast and I can do that because I'm a math whiz, so I got the job!

PETER: Cool. What kinda system?

MIRA: Well, if people get mad about being towed there are certain rules. Like if they use the S-word, I tell them there's an extra $20 charge for towing during rush hour. And if they use the F-word, I tell them there's an extra $50 charge for having to break into their car to put it into neutral. And if they *physically* threaten me, I just push this secret button under my desk and before Tom brings the car up from the lot, he puts a dent in it with a baseball bat. Isn't that clever? And there are all sorts of other extra charges that depend on other types of behavior. It's like combining psychology and math! I evaluate their mental condition, then charge 'em for it! Isn't that a great system?

CLAIRE: Very clever, sweetie.

PETER: Yeah. That's cool, Mom. What's for dinner?

MIRA: I thought we'd go out to dinner. To celebrate.

PETER: Cool. I want a burger.

MIRA: Hamburger Heaven! Let's go!

PETER: Oh, wait. I gotta ask you guys an important question before we go. Maybe I should get a snack.

MIRA: Okay.

(PETER exits to get another snack.)

CLAIRE: I'm so proud of you, sweetie.

(CLAIRE tries to hug MIRA. MIRA pushes her away.)

MIRA: Look. I'm being civil to you for Peter's sake. Don't touch me. And will you please stop calling me 'sweetie'?

CLAIRE: No, I won't. We need to deal with this!

MIRA: Tell me she didn't have washboard abs and perky breasts.

CLAIRE: Look, just talk this out with me, or—

MIRA: Or what, Claire? You'll start cruising chicks at the Humane Society?

CLAIRE: Stop it, Mira.

MIRA: Or you'll start hanging out at a petting zoo looking for a new housewife?

CLAIRE: Stop it, goddammit!

(PETER enters eating something.)

PETER: Are you fighting again?

CLAIRE: No.

MIRA: Yes.

PETER: Do you want me to leave?

MIRA: No, honey. You have an important question.

PETER: Yeah. Okay. So...who's my father?

MIRA: You don't have one.

PETER: Dude, that is totally impossible.

CLAIRE: Peter, you don't have a father, you have a *sperm donor*.

PETER: Okay, I'll buy that. Who's my sperm donor?

CLAIRE: We don't know. Donors are anonymous.

PETER: Can I find out who he was?

MIRA: No.

CLAIRE: Yes.

MIRA: Yes?

CLAIRE: Yes. We have what's called a "yes" donor. Someone who will allow his records to be unsealed at the time of his child's eighteenth birthday.

MIRA: We do?

CLAIRE: Didn't you read the contract?

MIRA: No. That was your job.

CLAIRE: Well, anyway—

PETER: Whoa. So like in a few days I can ask for the records?

CLAIRE: Yes.

MIRA: No!

CLAIRE: Yes.

MIRA: Boy, Claire, I'd say you're battin' a thousand around here.

CLAIRE: *(ignoring her)* I'll give you the number of the clinic.

MIRA: I don't believe this. Why do you want to know?

PETER: Just curious. I need my medical history. Paige was saying that like what if my father—

CLAIRE: Sperm donor.

PETER: What if my sperm donor had a history of some weird illness...

MIRA: Then they wouldn't let him donate sperm...

CLAIRE: They're pretty careful about that stuff, Peter. They only allow men with very healthy backgrounds to donate.

PETER: Yeah, but what if in the meantime *his* father died of some rare blood disease or some weird cancer or something? Medical histories can change, you know.

CLAIRE: Do you want to meet this man, or just get his medical history?

PETER: Well, I wouldn't mind meeting him, I guess. Maybe I look like him. I don't really look like you guys.

MIRA: You look like you.

PETER: Fuckin-A, Mom. Wouldn't you be curious?

MIRA: No.

PETER: I'm not gonna run away and live with him. I just want to meet him.

MIRA: So Paige put you up to this?

PETER: No.

MIRA: You've never asked before.

PETER: Never thought much about it before.

MIRA: But Paige thought about it, didn't she?

CLAIRE: Mira, it's okay...

MIRA: Hussy!

PETER: Fuckin-A, Mom. That's pretty harsh.

CLAIRE: Let's just go to dinner, shall we?

MIRA: Shall we invite *Paige?* Maybe she has more things for us all to worry about. I find these sorts of discussions are particularly helpful for the digestion.

PETER: God, Mom! What's the big deal?

MIRA: What's wrong, Peter? Aren't we good enough for you now that you're becoming a man? You need someone around with a penis, is that it?

PETER: Whoa, Mom. You are way outta line.

MIRA: No, *you're* out of line! I am your mother!

CLAIRE: Mira—

MIRA: Stay out of this! How do you think it makes me feel with you running around looking for another parent?

PETER: Well, how do you think it makes me feel to know I *have* another parent out there that I've never met?!

MIRA: He is not a goddamned parent! You call sperm a parent? Is that what a parent is to you, Peter? Sperm?!

PETER: I'm just talking about the biology, Mother!

CLAIRE: Mira, I don't see why—

MIRA: Shut up!

CLAIRE: Don't tell me to shut up—

MIRA: *(ignoring CLAIRE)* A parent is someone who changes your diapers and bandages your scrapes and wipes your tears and your nose and feeds you and puts up with you when you're being a jerk!! Do you think that's how Sperm-man feels? Do you?

PETER: Don't call him that.

MIRA: I'll call him whatever I want to!

PETER: Fuck you.

(MIRA slaps PETER's face. PETER just stares at her. His lip quivers, he's about to start crying.)

CLAIRE: Jesus, Mira...

MIRA: Don't you *ever* speak to me like that! *(heading out)* I'm going out.

(MIRA stomps off. PETER sniffles and CLAIRE goes to him.)

CLAIRE: Oh, sweetie, I'm so sorry. She didn't mean to hit you.

PETER: *(rubbing his cheek)* Sure feels like she meant to.

CLAIRE: She's just upset lately...she's mad at me about something and she's taking it out on you...

PETER: Yeah, well you must've done something pretty bad, 'cause she's never hit me before.

CLAIRE: I'm sorry...

PETER: What'd you do?

CLAIRE: You don't wanna know that stuff. Remember?

PETER: Whatever. Just don't do it again, or I'll end up with a black eye.

CLAIRE: I won't. You want to go get some dinner?

PETER: I'm not hungry. I'm gonna go take a walk. Maybe I'll go over to Paige's.

CLAIRE: Okay.

PETER: 'Night.

CLAIRE: Love you. I'm sorry about...

PETER: Whatever.

(PETER exits. CLAIRE sits on the sofa and stares into space. The phone rings. CLAIRE glances toward it, but doesn't move to answer it. It rings and rings and rings....)

BLACKOUT.

Scene Two

(Evening. Peter's birthday. PETER is on the phone. He looks upset.)

PETER: But, I— ... But—... Uh-huh...Okay. Bye.

(PETER hangs up. MIRA enters unnoticed. She is carrying a birthday cake in a box.)

PETER: Fuckin-A. Happy Birthday to me.

MIRA: Hey there.

(PETER jumps.)

PETER: Hey, Mom.

MIRA: You okay, sweetie?

PETER: Yeah, I'm fine...you scared me.

MIRA: Sorry. What's up?

PETER: Nothing.

MIRA: Yes there is.

PETER: No there's not.

MIRA: Yes there is. I can tell. I can always tell.

PETER: I'm fine!

(MIRA eyes him suspiciously.)

MIRA: *(touching his cheek)* Peter, we used to talk... I don't understand what's happening to you lately.

PETER: Me? What's happening to *you?* It's like you're mad all the time. You're mad at me about the sperm donor thing and you're mad at Mom about that and something else.

MIRA: I have a pretty good reason.

PETER: Fine. Don't listen to me, I'm just a stupid kid! Just walk around here mad and make everyone miserable and hit people! Whatever.

MIRA: I'm so sorry about that Peter.

PETER: Whatever. It's like walking in a minefield around here. So whatever it is, just get over it, Mom.

MIRA: Is that what you do, Peter? Whenever you have a problem, you just "get over it?"

PETER: No, Mom. I *talk* about it, because you *make* me talk about it. So *talk* to Mom!

MIRA: It's not quite that simple!

(The phone rings. MIRA answers it.)

MIRA: Hello?...Hello?....Look, I don't know who you are, but— Oh, God, wait— I *do* know who you are! You listen here you little— Hello?

(MIRA hangs up the phone. She is shaking.)

PETER: What was that about?

MIRA: *That* is why I'm mad at your mother.

PETER: Because some psycho keeps calling us?

MIRA: Your mother had an affair.

PETER: What?

MIRA: I said—

PETER: I heard what you said! Why the hell did you tell me that?!! Oh, God!!! I can't believe you just told me that!! I don't wanna know that stuff!!! Fuckin-A, Mom!

(MIRA starts to cry. PETER is hopping around, grabbing his hair, trying to erase this information from his brain.)

PETER: Shit! God! Aw, Mom. Don't cry. God!

(PETER pats her on the shoulder awkwardly.)

PETER: It's okay, Mom. Don't cry. Please? Shit! God!

MIRA: I'm sorry.

PETER: It's okay.

MIRA: I shouldn't have told you that—

PETER: It's okay.

MIRA: You're right. I should talk to her and—

PETER: Can we please stop talking about this?!

MIRA: Sorry. Umm.... What time is Paige coming over?

PETER: In about an hour.

MIRA: We'll have your cake when she gets here, then get out of the way.

PETER: Okay. So...um...where are the...uh...?

MIRA: What?—oh. You'll get them when you open the rest of your presents.

PETER: Can't I just look at them? I've never really seen one up close.

MIRA: Do you know how to put one on?

PETER: Won't it be obvious?

MIRA: I don't know. You should read the instructions.

PETER: I don't wanna sit and read the instructions in front of Paige.

MIRA: I guess you should have them now.

PETER: Yeah, then I could get used to them. This is making me nervous...

(MIRA retrieves a small gift-wrapped box and hands it to PETER.)

PETER: You didn't need to wrap 'em, Mom...

MIRA: It's your birthday.

(PETER tears off the wrapping and studies his brand new box of condoms.)

MIRA: I hope they're the right kind. There were some that were extra large. You're not extra large, are you?

PETER: *(opening the box and pulling out the instructions)* I don't think so.

MIRA: Do you like them?

PETER: Totally. Thanks a lot, Mom.

(MIRA runs off briefly, then runs back on carrying a large zucchini, which she hands to PETER.)

MIRA: Here. Practice with this. Then you won't get nervous later.

PETER: Okay.

(PETER wanders off, holding the carrot and reading the instructions. CLAIRE enters with a large box.)

CLAIRE: Where's Peter?

MIRA: He's practicing his condoms.

CLAIRE: Oh. Have you been crying?

MIRA: We can talk about it later.

CLAIRE: Okay.

MIRA: Did you get it?

CLAIRE: Well...no...I got him something different.

MIRA: Without asking me?

CLAIRE: Don't get mad. It was a spur of the moment sort of thing.

MIRA: Lemme see.

(CLAIRE takes the lid off the box and MIRA looks inside.)

MIRA: Wow.

CLAIRE: Is it okay?

MIRA: He'll love it. Are you sure about this?

CLAIRE: Yeah, I'm sure. Is it okay with you?

MIRA: It's the perfect present. Let's give it to him.

CLAIRE: Okay.

MIRA: Peter!

PETER: *(off stage)* Just a sec!

MIRA: How'd you get it home?

CLAIRE: Paige brought it. She's out there now. I called her and she came and helped me pick it out.

MIRA: Oh, did she now? How sweet.

CLAIRE: She's really a very nice girl, Mira.

MIRA: She's a troublemaker.

CLAIRE: Well, Peter likes her and we owe it to him to like her too.

MIRA: Hmph.

(PETER enters holding a condom-encased zucchini. He behaves coolly toward CLAIRE throughout the following.)

PETER: *(waving the carrot)* Think I got it. Oh, hi Mom.

CLAIRE: *(holding out the box)* Happy Birthday!

PETER: Thanks. Can I open it now?

MIRA: You *may*.

(PETER takes the lid off the box and looks into it. His eyes get very big.)

PETER: Holy shit! Are you serious?

MIRA: Yes.

PETER: Where is it?!

CLAIRE: In the driveway.

PETER: Whoa.

(PETER pulls a motorcycle helmet out of the box. He's completely spastic and tears off stage.)

PETER: Thanks Moms!

(PETER finds PAIGE wheeling out his new bike. Throughout the following, PETER checks out the bike, etc.

Pause. MIRA looks at CLAIRE expectantly.)

CLAIRE: What now?

MIRA: Well?

CLAIRE: Well, what?

MIRA: Aren't you even going to ask me? See? That is so typical of you. Do you see what I'm talking about?

CLAIRE: What've I done now?—Oh my God! Your first day at work! How was it?

MIRA: It was really fun!

CLAIRE: Yeah?

MIRA: It was great! There are a lot of angry people out there, let me tell you... I was racking up charges right and left. Tom was thrilled. He said I'd made more money on my first day than the last woman did in a week!

CLAIRE: That's great.

MIRA: And on my lunch hour I picked up the cutest curtains at K-Mart for the trailer. It makes all the difference. Tom liked them a lot.

CLAIRE: That's great, honey.

MIRA: How was your day?

CLAIRE: Quiet. A couple of neuterings, a teeth cleaning, and a Husky who swallowed a pair of socks.

MIRA: This is kinda fun. Talking about our jobs. It's so grown-up.

CLAIRE: Yeah...it is...it's kinda...sexy.

MIRA: Don't use that word around me.

CLAIRE: She weighed seven hundred pounds and had long, greasy, black hair.

MIRA: You think that's funny?

CLAIRE: No, I just... No...nothing's funny. I don't know what to say... I love you, Mira.

MIRA: Duh, Claire.

(CLAIRE can't help but laugh. She puts a hand on Mira's knee. MIRA shies away and CLAIRE takes her hand away.)

MIRA: I don't trust you anymore.

CLAIRE: Can you trust me enough to take you to dinner?

MIRA: I suppose.

(They rise and head out.)

CLAIRE: Oh, wait, we have to have Peter's cake first.

MIRA: Oh, Claire, Claire, Claire. Peter's got a motorcycle, a girl, and a brand-new box of condoms...the cake can wait.

CLAIRE: Yeah, I guess you're right.

(They exit and reappear by the bike. They go to PETER who is sitting on his new bike.)

CLAIRE: What do you think? Pretty spiffy, huh?

PETER: *(shrugs)* Yeah.

MIRA: Peter, don't be rude...

PETER: *(forced smile toward CLAIRE)* Thanks, mom.

CLAIRE: *(completely confused)* You're welcome.

(MIRA pulls CLAIRE off stage.)

CLAIRE: What was that about?

PAIGE: *(waving to them)* 'Night.

(CLAIRE and MIRA are gone. PETER and PAIGE head back inside.)

PAIGE: So anyway, the sperm dude...

PETER: I only talked to him for a little bit...

PAIGE: And?

(PETER shrugs. He starts to cry. PAIGE holds him.)

PAIGE: What's the matter?

PETER: He said he doesn't want to meet me. He said he'd send me his medical history, but he thinks it's best if we don't meet. And he said his wife doesn't want him to meet me and he had to honor her wishes and shit like that.

PAIGE: Phht! What a dickhead. Dude, I'm so sorry.

PETER: It's okay. Doesn't matter.

PAIGE: Fuckin-A.

PETER: It's okay. I mean it's not like I'm his son or anything. I was just curious to see what he looks like. I never thought about it before and now I think about it all the time.

PAIGE: That's my fault. I shouldn't have bugged you about it.

PETER: Nah, I would've thought about it on my own sooner or later.

(PETER disentangles himself and wipes his nose on his sleeve.)

PAIGE: I can't believe him. What a dickhead. Fuckin-A. I mean why is he a "yes" donor if he's just gonna say "no"?

PETER: He said, "Things change." But he also said that he thinks I should have my medical history and that's mostly why he became a "yes" donor in the first place. He's gonna mail it to me.

PAIGE: Well, isn't that swell of him.

PETER: Well, at least I have that. I could've had a total "no" donor.

PAIGE: What a dickhead. Fuckin-A.

PETER: Isn't it weird that guys can have kids they've never seen? Girls can't do that.

PAIGE: Yeah.

PETER: I mean I can make life just by...by...you know...but you can only make life by carrying it all around for nine months. It's like you're making soup and I would just be one of the ingredients, but you would be the soup pot. That's weird as shit! Fuckin-A...

PAIGE: It's totally not fair.

PETER: Not at all. But, you know it's also totally cool that you can do that. I wouldn't mind being able to do that...

(PAIGE lunges at PETER and kisses him.)

PETER: Whoa.

PAIGE: You are so cute.

PETER: Naw...

PAIGE: Yeah... Um, I really want to...

PETER: Me too...

PAIGE: When are your moms coming back?

PETER: Not 'til late.

PAIGE: Do you have the...?

PETER: Yeah, Mom bought me like a whole case of 'em.

(They embrace and kiss passionately.)

BLACKOUT

Scene Three

(Late that night. The stage is lit only dimly. PETER sits alone in the living room. He has a nearly-empty cakeplate on his lap and is finishing it up with a fork. He looks depressed. MIRA and CLAIRE enter, stumbling over things. They fumble for the lights and do not see PETER.)

CLAIRE: Sh, sh! They might still be—

PETER: We're not.

(CLAIRE and MIRA scream.)

CLAIRE: Oh my God! I didn't see you!

PETER: You didn't wait for cake.

CLAIRE: What—? You were busy with Paige and the new bike and we figured we could eat it later.

PETER: I already ate it.

MIRA: Well, let's have some more.

PETER: I ate all of it.

MIRA: You ate the whole cake?

PETER: I didn't know when you were coming home, if ever. Are you still fighting?

MIRA: Not at the moment.

CLAIRE: *(turning the lights up a little brighter)* Peter, what's the matter?

MIRA: Did you have a good time? Was it...fun?...was it what you thought it would be?

PETER: I'm still a virgin.

MIRA: What? Why? Did Paige change her mind, that—

PETER: I couldn't get it up.

MIRA: Oh.

CLAIRE: That happens sometimes, sweetie, it's nothing to worry about...

(CLAIRE isn't actually sure if that happens, she shrugs and looks to MIRA for help. MIRA nods.)

PETER: But I've had at least five erections a day since I was thirteen!

MIRA: I'm sure it was just nerves. Don't take it so hard.

PETER: Maybe I'm gay.

CLAIRE: Do you think you are?

PETER: I don't know. I must be.

CLAIRE: Are you attracted to other boys? Men?

PETER: No.

CLAIRE: But you're attracted to girls?

PETER: I thought I was...

CLAIRE: Peter, you mustn't make such a big deal out of this.

(PETER shrugs.)

MIRA: Paige was okay with it, wasn't she?

PETER: I guess. I don't know. I started crying and I think it wigged her out and she left.

MIRA: She just left without saying anything? That—

PETER: She said I was making a big deal out of it.

MIRA: Oh. Well, she's right. I remember I had this boyfriend in high school who—

PETER: God, Mom! How many times do I have to tell you? I don't wanna know that stuff!

MIRA: Sorry.

PETER: I'm going to bed. Thanks for the bike. It's totally awesome.

CLAIRE: Good night dear.

(PETER exits.)

MIRA: Poor guy. Peter's peter petered out and performed poorly.

(MIRA and CLAIRE collapse on the couch, laughing.)

BLACKOUT

Scene Four

(The next day An empty living room. PETER's motorcycle helmet sits on the coffee table. CLAIRE enters with a large box.)

CLAIRE: Hello?! Anybody here?

(CLAIRE hides the box behind the couch as PETER enters wearing an apron and an oven mitt.)

PETER: Hi Mom. How was work?

CLAIRE: Great. I saved a horse's life today!

PETER: Cool. What's in the box?

CLAIRE: A present for your Mom.

PETER: 'Cause she's so pissed about the affair?

(CLAIRE is quite taken aback.)

CLAIRE: What did you say?

PETER: You heard me.

CLAIRE: I'm sorry your mother told you that.

PETER: Me too. But that was way uncool of you.

CLAIRE: It was. But how about we talk about this when you're forty?

PETER: Phht!

CLAIRE: I'm sorry. Do you want to talk about it now?

(The phone rings. They both look at the phone, but do not move to get it. They look at one another.)

PETER: Don't you want to get that?

CLAIRE: No.

PETER: *(moving toward the phone)* I bet.

CLAIRE: Peter—

(PETER picks up the receiver and immediately drops it back into the cradle without putting it to his ear. He watches CLAIRE the whole time.)

CLAIRE: I'm sorry.

PETER: You messed everything up around here. First, you were hardly ever around all summer because you were "working" so much—yeah, right—and now Mom went and got a job because she's mad at you, so *no one's* ever around!

CLAIRE: Look, Peter, I don't you want you to worry about this. We'll get through it and we'll always be here for you. Together.

PETER: Promise?

CLAIRE: Give it some time, sweetie. *(smiling, trying to jolly him up)* Just promise me you won't run away and live with your sperm donor or something—

(PETER's eyes well up and looks like he's about to cry.)

CLAIRE: It was just a joke.

PETER: I talked to him.

CLAIRE: You did? I didn't know you even had his number. What's his name?

PETER: Harold Carter. Is Harold like the stupidest name there is or what?

CLAIRE: Well, what did he say?

PETER: He won't meet me.

CLAIRE: He won't? Why not?

PETER: What do you care?

CLAIRE: I care a lot. I think you should meet him.

PETER: Yeah, right.

CLAIRE: Who signed the contract, Peter? *(no response)* Who?

PETER: *(quietly)* You.

CLAIRE: That's right. *(she gives him a hug)* Why are you wearing an apron?

PETER: I'm making dinner.

CLAIRE: Oh. Why?

PETER: Because no one else was.

CLAIRE: Ah. How lovely. Thank you, Peter.

PETER: You're welcome.

CLAIRE: How are you doing that?

PETER: What?

CLAIRE: Making dinner.

PETER: Duh, Mom. I'm following a cookbook. I'm eighteen. I can read now.

MIRA: *(from off-stage)* Hello?

PETER: Can we tell Mom about the Harold thing later? She'd probably be all happy that he won't meet me and I can't deal with that right now.

CLAIRE: Okay.

(PETER exits. MIRA enters.)

MIRA: Hi.

CLAIRE: Why did you tell him?

MIRA: What? Oh.

CLAIRE: That was out of bounds.

MIRA: I'm sorry...it just slipped out. I was upset.

CLAIRE: This has nothing to do with Peter.

MIRA: I know. You're right. I'm sorry. I'm so sorry.

(PETER enters looking for his oven mitt.)

PETER: Hi Mom. How was work?

MIRA: I got fired.

PETER: Bummer.

CLAIRE: Fired?! Why? Tom loves you!

MIRA: I fed the dogs.

CLAIRE: You what?

MIRA: Tom has these two Dobermans. I thought they seemed awfully testy and so I figured they might just be hungry. They looked a little skinny to me...so anyway, the other day I picked up a bag of dog food on my way to work and you should have seen them go at it! So for the past couple days I've been feeding them and let me tell you they've been a lot more pleasant to be around! They've been hanging out with me in my trailer...you know, just snoozing, I mean that's what dogs do, don't they?...and then today Tom walks in and sees Slasher and Basher asleep by my desk and he goes ballistic!

CLAIRE: Mira, I think the idea is that—

MIRA: You know why he has those dogs?

CLAIRE: To guard the lot.

MIRA: To guard the lot! And he tells me they won't guard the lot if they're all fat and happy and he can't believe I'm *feeding* them. And he said that last night four cars were taken out of the lot and now he knows why! Like it's my fault! I mean we're a pretty high-tech country...Hungry Dogs is kind of a primitive security system, don't you think?

PETER: It's pretty common practice...

MIRA: To starve dogs?

PETER: So they'll be meaner.

MIRA: That's disgusting.

CLAIRE: Yes, it is.

PETER: What happened to them?

MIRA: I called the Humane Society after Tom fired me.

PETER: Go Mom.

CLAIRE: Good for you.

(MIRA looks at Peter.)

MIRA: Why are you wearing an apron?

CLAIRE: He's making dinner.

MIRA: Really? Why?

PETER: No one else was. Oh yeah, and Paige is coming over.

CLAIRE: Great.

MIRA: Uh-huh. What are you making?

PETER: Pot Roast.

MIRA: Yum! You found my Fannie Farmer Cookbook, didn't you?

PETER: Yeah. It seemed like the easiest one.

MIRA: It is. A well-written cookbook, that one. Good choice.

PETER: Thanks. I gotta go check on it.

PETER exits.

CLAIRE: I'm sorry about your job, sweetie.

MIRA: I'm sorry I told Peter about your... the...you know...

CLAIRE: I'm sorry about the...you know...

MIRA: We're a pretty sorry pair, aren't we? Come talk to me while I get out of these clothes.

(They exit. After a moment, the doorbell rings.)

PETER: *(off stage)* I'll get it!

(PETER enters with PAIGE, who carries her helmet.)

PAIGE: Nice apron, dude.

PETER: I'm making dinner.

PAIGE: Cool.

(They sit on the couch. Awkward pause.)

PETER: Thanks for ditching school with me today. I had a nice time.

PAIGE: Don't be so weird, it was fuckin' amazing!

PETER: Yeah, I guess it was.

PAIGE: My friend Carla-May was saying that the first time for girls wasn't so great, but I totally had a great time.

PETER: Totally.

(They kiss. MIRA enters, straightening out her clothing.)

MIRA: Oops! Sorry, kids.

(PETER breaks away from PAIGE.)

PETER: No prob.

(Something occurs to MIRA as she looks from PETER to PAIGE and back. While she is scrutinizing them, CLAIRE enters.)

MIRA: Look at them!

CLAIRE: What?

PETER: Mom...

PAIGE: What?

MIRA: Am I right?

PETER: Yeah, yeah. Old news.

CLAIRE: What are you talking about?

PETER: Nothing.

MIRA: Can't you see?! Peter's lost his virginity!

PETER: Fuckin-A...

CLAIRE: Ohhhh! Yes, now I see it. Well, congratulations, dear.

PETER: Maaaaaaaa!

PAIGE: I am totally mortified.

MIRA: Was it fun?

PETER: Maaaaaaaa!

PAIGE: I can't even make eye contact, I am so mortified.

CLAIRE: Don't be silly, Paige. Look at me....c'mon...look at me....Paaaaaige....talk to me Paige.

PAIGE: Hey Dr. Gray, Mrs. Gray.

MIRA: Hey.

CLAIRE: That's better. How are you, dear?

PAIGE: Fine. I'm great. I'm fine.

PETER: Fuckin-A, I gotta check the roast.

(PETER exits.)

CLAIRE: Have a seat, Paige.

(The women all sit.)

PAIGE: So whaddaya think about this dickhead?—sorry—*guy*.

MIRA: What guy?

PAIGE: Peter's sperm donor.

CLAIRE: Mrs. Gray just got home, she hasn't heard the news.

PAIGE: Oh, sorry.

MIRA: What news?

CLAIRE: Peter's sperm donor refuses to meet him.

MIRA: Why?

PAIGE: "Things change."

MIRA: Is Peter upset?

PAIGE & CLAIRE: Yes.

CLAIRE: He cried.

MIRA: He cried?

PAIGE & CLAIRE: Yes.

MIRA: Why didn't he tell me?

CLAIRE: You just got home—

MIRA: Why didn't *you* tell me?

CLAIRE: Mira, you weren't exactly thrilled about the whole thing...

MIRA: What?...but that doesn't mean... I mean...I want what Peter wants...he's my son—I can't believe he won't meet Peter! What a jerk...what a ....

PAIGE: Dickhead.

MIRA: Right. Peter is a wonderful kid! Why the hell won't he meet him?

CLAIRE: I don't know...he just won't.

PAIGE: Part of it's 'cause of his wife.

MIRA: Phht! What a...

PAIGE: Dickhead.

MIRA: Right. The nerve of this guy! What? He just wants to ejaculate into a dixie cup and not deal with the results? What is that all about? What a...

PAIGE: Dickhead.

MIRA: Right.

CLAIRE: Mira, you didn't even want them to meet!

MIRA: But what right does this guy have to make my son cry? What right does he have to just refuse to meet such a beautiful boy? He signed a "yes" contract!

PAIGE: Yeah, and then he says "no." What a—

MIRA: Dickhead!

PAIGE: Right. Peter's totally upset.

MIRA: Well, we'll just have to do something about that...

(MIRA gets a positively diabolical gleam in her eye.)

CLAIRE: You have a plan, don't you?

MIRA: I think so. I'd need your help.

CLAIRE: Okay.

MIRA: You too, Paige.

PAIGE: Okay.

(PETER enters in his apron. The three women turn toward him and smile hugely.)

PETER: It's almost ready. What? What are you staring at?

BLACKOUT

Scene Five

(The living room is empty. MIRA tiptoes in, She looks around. Listens. She hears nothing.)

MIRA: *(whispering loudly)* Coast clear! Come on!

CLAIRE: *(off stage)* You have to help me!

MIRA: Right.

(MIRA runs back off. MIRA and CLAIRE enter shortly thereafter, carrying the inert body of HAROLD. He's wearing the fur-covered handcuffs from Act One. HAROLD looks more like PETER than either of the women do.)

CLAIRE: Where should we put him?

MIRA: I don't know. How long 'til he wakes up?

CLAIRE: I'm not sure.

MIRA: You're not sure? You're a doctor, you're supposed to know these things!

CLAIRE: I'm a *vet*! I gave him the dosage for a Great Dane. I didn't think he'd stay under even this long.

MIRA: You didn't kill him, did you?

CLAIRE: Can we just put him down?

MIRA: On the couch.

(They trundle him over to the couch and dump him onto it.)

CLAIRE: Do you think he'll be mad when he wakes up?

MIRA: *If* he wakes up...

CLAIRE: He was pretty mad when I gave him the shot...

MIRA: He was just surprised. He's drooling on the cushions.

CLAIRE: Drool is a good sign. Means his body is functioning normally again.

(They hear the sound of Peter's motorcycle pulling up and toss HAROLD over the back of the couch to hide him.)

PETER: *(off-stage)* Hello?!

(PETER and PAIGE enter the living room, carrying their respective motorcycle helmets.)

PETER: Hi Moms.

MIRA: Hello, dear.

PETER: Paige is here.

MIRA: I see that.

PAIGE: Hi.

MIRA: Hi.

PETER: Can she stay for dinner?

MIRA: She *may*.

PETER: What's for dinner?

MIRA: Whatever you want. Pizza?

PETER: Cool. Why are you acting so weird?

MIRA: *(signaling to PAIGE to get PETER out of the room)* I'm not.

PAIGE: C'mon, dude. Let's go to your room.

PETER: Okay.

(HAROLD starts to stir behind the couch. The women resettle themselves on the couch and make noises (coughing, etc) in an attempt to mask HAROLD's movements.)

CLAIRE: Don't...um...don't start anything...

PETER: Fuckin-A, Mom...

CLAIRE: We have a surprise for you and it'll be ready soon, so I'm just saying...

PETER: You're acting totally weird. C'mon Paige.

(PETER and PAIGE exit. HAROLD lets out a loud groan. They drag him from behind the couch.)

MIRA: It's alive.

CLAIRE: Thank heavens.

MIRA: Harold? Harold, can you hear me?

HAROLD: *(groggily)* Fuckin-A! Where am I?

CLAIRE: You're here, Harold. With Claire and Mira Gray.

HAROLD: Who're they?

CLAIRE: They're us, Harold.

HAROLD: Don't call me Harold.

CLAIRE: Mr. Carter, we—

HAROLD: Hal.

CLAIRE: Hal, we're not going to hurt you—

HAROLD: *(noticing the handcuffs and starting to panic)* What the—? Who the fuck are you?

CLAIRE: We're Peter's parents.

HAROLD: Peter? Oh, shit...the kid who called me.

CLAIRE: Correct. The result of your sperm donation, for which we are eternally grateful, but now we just have one more favor to ask...

HAROLD: Where is he?

MIRA: In his room.

HAROLD: Did he see me like this?

MIRA: No.

(HAROLD is a little more focused now. He struggles against the handcuffs and tries to rise. They push him back down.)

HAROLD: You kidnapped me! That's a federal offense!

MIRA: Yes, Hal, it is. But try to see things from our point of view—

HAROLD: And you drugged me! That's assault and battery!

MIRA: Not necessarily. She's a doctor.

HAROLD: Oh.

CLAIRE: I'm a vet.

MIRA: Claire...

HAROLD: A vet?!! Fuckin-A! A *vet?!!!*

CLAIRE: It's harder to get into vet school than med school, you know.

MIRA: Claire...

HAROLD: I want you take off these handcuffs right this second!

MIRA: I'll take them off if you'll agree to meet Peter.

HAROLD: I don't wanna meet Peter.

MIRA: Then why were you donating sperm?

HAROLD: I needed money. I was in college.

MIRA: So why did you sign on as a "yes" donor?

HAROLD: Because... I don't know...things were difficult back then..I let my emotions decide for me...I thought...I thought that kids should know who their parents are...I ...but...*things change* ...and I still want him to know his medical history, but not *me*.

MIRA: I'm not following.

HAROLD: I'm an orphan.

MIRA: What?

HAROLD: That's why I signed the "yes" contract. At the time, I figured if I had kids somewhere they would feel like orphans if they didn't know who I was and I didn't want them to feel like that because I always felt like that because I *was* an orphan. But *things change.*

CLAIRE: I wouldn't think they'd let orphans donate. You don't have the medical history...

HAROLD: I lied.

CLAIRE: You lied.

HAROLD: Well, I didn't actually lie, I just didn't tell them. They didn't ask outright. Well, sort of...but not really...Mostly they were just interested in my sperm count and my IQ. I have a high IQ. Anyway, I'm healthy.

MIRA: But how do we know you'll stay that way?

HAROLD: How do we know *you* will?

MIRA: It's not fair to Peter.

HAROLD: Water under the bridge. What do you want, a refund? I've survived with less knowledge than Peter will have. Would you please remove these handcuffs? I'm allergic to fur.

(HAROLD sniffles to prove his point.)

MIRA: It's not real fur.

HAROLD: Oh.

CLAIRE: You're allergic to animals?

HAROLD: Yes.

CLAIRE: Figures.

HAROLD: Could I at least call my wife? I'm usually home by now. She'll probably be calling the police soon and then you'll be in big trouble—hey, how am I gonna get out of here anyway?

MIRA: I drove your car here. We took your keys after you passed out.

HAROLD: Oh.

CLAIRE: Promise to meet Peter and you can call your wife.

HAROLD: I don't wanna meet him.

CLAIRE: I think you do.

HAROLD: Of course I do! But I promised my wife...

CLAIRE: Your wife isn't here.

HAROLD: A promise is a promise.

CLAIRE: Does she have a promise in writing...like Peter does?

(HAROLD sighs, defeated.)

HAROLD: Fine. I'll meet him. Briefly.

CLAIRE: Okay.

HAROLD: *Briefly.*

CLAIRE: Fine.

MIRA: *(handing him the phone)* No funny stuff. Any funny stuff and she shoots you up again. Got it?

HAROLD: Got it. *(he dials, with some difficulty)* Hi, Cookie.

MIRA: Cookie?

HAROLD: I'm gonna be a little late. I'm, uh...over at some friends' house....no, you don't know them...I met them at the office today... well, I sort of met them in the parking lot...Yes, it is a strange place to meet people, an entirely new experience for me, but maybe I could explain it later? Hm? Uh, Claire and...and...

MIRA: *(whispering)* Mira.

HAROLD: Claire and Mira. Hm? Yes....uh-huh... I'll be home in about... *(he looks to CLAIRE and MIRA for help, MIRA holds up one finger)* ...in about an hour...Uh-huh. Good...What's for dinner?...God, you know I hate brussel sprouts. Okay. Sorry. No. Right. Uh-huh. No. Yeah... Well, I'll tell you whole fascinating story when I get home, okay? Bye-bye, Boo-Boo. See you soon.

(He hangs up.)

MIRA: Peter hates brussel sprouts too.

HAROLD: Who doesn't?

MIRA: Why doesn't your wife want you to meet Peter?

HAROLD: It's an uncomfortable situation for her.

MIRA: Do you and your wife have children?

HAROLD: She can't have children.

MIRA: Oh, God, I'm so sorry—

MIRA: God, that must be terrible for your wife knowing that you've got a—

HAROLD: Look, I said I'd meet Peter. Let me meet him and go home.

(MIRA takes a key from her pocket and starts to uncuff HAROLD.)

MIRA: He's a great kid, I think you'll really like him.

HAROLD: Uh-huh. *(he stretches out his freed wrists)* Thank you.

MIRA: I'll call Peter. Oh, this is so exciting. PETER!!!!

PETER: *(off-stage)* What?

MIRA: Your surprise is ready!!!!

PETER: *(off-stage)* Be out in a minute!

MIRA: No. *Now!!!*

PETER: *(off-stage)* Fuckin-A, Mom!!!

MIRA: NOW!!!

(PETER and PAIGE enter looking rumpled PETER notices HAROLD. HAROLD stands. He looks miserable.)

PETER: Whoa.

MIRA: Peter, this is—

PETER: Harold.

HAROLD: Hal.

PETER: Hal.

MIRA: How'd you know?

PETER: He looks like me. Or moves like me. Or something...

HAROLD: *(holding out his hand, which PETER shakes)* It's nice to meet you, Peter.

PETER: You too..um...this is my girlfriend, Paige.

HAROLD: Hi.

PAIGE: Wow. Hi. This is so totally cool of you to do.

PETER: Yeah, thanks. I know you didn't want to.

HAROLD: Well, your...uh... *they* talked me into it.

PETER: Yeah?

CLAIRE: It was your Mom's idea.

PETER: Really?

MIRA: Really.

PETER: Wow. Well, hey, sit down. Are you staying for dinner?

HAROLD: No. My wife doesn't know I'm here and—

PETER: Oh, well, that's okay...

HAROLD: It's a little weird for her.

PETER: Yeah, I bet. I mean isn't it totally weird that guys can have kids they've never seen? Women can't do that.

HAROLD: Exactly. *(suddenly standing)* Well, it was nice meeting you all.

MIRA: Oh, have a seat, Hal. Stay a while longer. *(hissing)* Sit!

(HAROLD sits.)

MIRA: So...Hal was just telling us his wife can't have children.

HAROLD: Jesus—

PETER: Oh man, I'm really sorry, I mean, this must be really—

HAROLD: Could we talk about something else?

MIRA: Sure. Talk to Peter. You two need to...catch up.

HAROLD: Yeah...so, um...are you happy, Peter?

PETER: About what?

HAROLD: I don't know...with your life, I guess.

PETER: Oh. Well, sure...I guess... I mean I'm not one of those suicidal teenagers or anything...

HAROLD: Good, good.

PAIGE: What do you do for a living?

HAROLD: Oh, nothing exciting. I'm an engineer. I was always good at math, so...

PETER: I'm good at math too.

MIRA: I'm a math whiz.

HAROLD: Great, great. So you must be about to go to college.

PETER: Next year.

HAROLD: What do you want to study?

PETER: I dunno. Whatever.

HAROLD: Well, I'm sure you'll figure it out eventually. Don't rush it.

PETER: Okay.

CLAIRE: What sort of things do you like to do? When you're not engineering something...

HAROLD: Oh, this and that. I like to listen to music. Go to concerts.

PETER: Me too!

PAIGE: What's your all-time favorite album?

HAROLD: Um..let's see...probably Meatloaf's "Bat Out of Hell."

PETER: No way! That's mine!

HAROLD: No way!!

PETER: Way! It's an amazing album.

HAROLD: Truly amazing.

PETER: During "Paradise By the Dashboard Lights," when he does that baseball thing—

HAROLD: Oh, that's just so—

PETER: Sometimes I listen to it over and over—

HAROLD: Oh, me to. It's great.

PETER: Totally.

HAROLD: Yeah.

(They smile and nod. Awkward pause.)

HAROLD: *(starting to rise)* Well, I should—

MIRA: Don't you have something to tell Peter? Hal has something to tell you, Peter.

PETER: Okay.

HAROLD: I do?

MIRA: Your parents...

HAROLD: Oh, yeah. Um... I'm an orphan, Peter.

PETER: An orphan?

HAROLD: Well, you know...I was adopted and everything...

PAIGE: Whoa.

HAROLD: But I have no idea who my biological parents are, or *were*.

PAIGE: Whoa.

PETER: Whoa.

HAROLD: Sorry, but your history sort of starts and ends here as far as your paternal line goes.

PETER: Okay. That's cool. I can deal with that.

CLAIRE: But he's very healthy, Peter.

PETER: Yeah, that's cool. I don't even think about that medical stuff really, I was just wondering about...I dunno...I was just...*wondering*, I guess.

HAROLD: Yeah, tell me about it. I wonder all the time. It can drive you crazy.

PETER: Yeah.

HAROLD: Look, can I ask a question?

MIRA: You *may*.

HAROLD: I'm curious how this was done...

MIRA: Meaning "how was Peter done?"

HAROLD: Yeah, did you just walk into some fertility clinic and end up with my sperm?...or...I dunno...I don't know how it works...

CLAIRE: A friend of ours, Bill—

HAROLD: Doctor Bill! I remember Doctor Bill!

CLAIRE: Right. I went to school with him. We branched off, obviously. I inseminate horses, he inseminates women. Anyway, he was working on a new procedure... Peter, do you want Paige to hear this?

PAIGE: What? I wanna hear it. Can I hear it?

PETER: Yeah, it's okay.

CLAIRE: Okay. So we really wanted a child and to make a long story short, Mira gave physical birth to Peter, but we don't know whose biological child Peter is, because Doctor Bill inseminated Mira, but he also inseminated my eggs in his lab and implanted them in Mira at the same time.

HAROLD: Whoa.

PAIGE: Whoa.

CLAIRE: We have no idea which conception happened and we've never had a DNA test or anything to find out. Once we saw Peter, it didn't really matter. He was ours.

HAROLD: Whoa.

CLAIRE: I know that procedure happens more these days, but it was new back then.

HAROLD: That is so intense! I mean, you can just give someone your sperm and they can do all sorts of weird shit with it. Fuckin-A! What a trip!

PETER: A long trip.

MIRA: Isn't he the cutest?

HAROLD: He is. He really is.

PAIGE: Totally. And he looks like...

HAROLD: Like me. Yeah, he does, a little.

PETER: *God, you guys....*

HAROLD: I feel like crying.

(He puts his head in his hand and sniffles.)

PETER: Moms! Check it out.

CLAIRE: We're checking.

HAROLD: What?

PETER: I cry sooooo easily.

PAIGE: Totally.

HAROLD: *(wiping his eyes and lurching to his feet)* I have to go.

PETER: No.

HAROLD: I have to. Look, Peter, I have another life...

PETER: I know. But maybe we could get together sometime?

HAROLD: No.

PETER: No?

HAROLD: I don't think so.

PETER: You mean like *never*?

HAROLD: Right.

PETER: Fuckin-A. But I'm your...

HAROLD: You're not my son, Peter. Biologically you are, but realistically you're not.

PETER: But—

HAROLD: Look, I'm glad I got to meet you, but I didn't raise you and I can't start playing Dad with an eighteen-year-old. That's not fair to you, to me, to my wife, or to your...uh...moms. I just donated sperm. I needed money and I donated sperm.

PETER: Children! Sperm becomes children, dude! That is just so random to just give your children away.

HAROLD: Well, you wouldn't exactly be here if I hadn't!

PETER: I just think it's pretty irresponsible...

HAROLD: Are you listening to me? You wouldn't be here! And maybe some other couple wouldn't have a kid if I hadn't donated!

CLAIRE: He's right Peter. You wouldn't be here if he hadn't donated sperm.

PETER: WELL MAYBE I DON'T CARE IF I WOULDN'T BE HERE!

(MIRA, CLAIRE, and PAIGE took at him with expressions of utter horror. PETER realizes what he has said, and starts to cry. HAROLD reaches for him, then checks himself. MIRA, CLAIRE, and PAIGE do the same.)

HAROLD: This is very hard for me, Peter. Part of me wants to give you a big hug and sit and talk to you for hours. God, it's fascinating for me just to look at you! But you're not my son and I have to go on with my life and you have to go on with yours.

PAIGE: What about if you just got together once in a while and...played football or something—

CLAIRE: *We* play football with him...

HAROLD: No.

PETER: It's okay, guys. He doesn't wanna see me.

HAROLD: I *do* want to see you...

MIRA: So how can you just—?

PETER: It's *okay*! He's right. He's not my father. I don't even know what I was expecting. I don't even need a father...it's just so weird.

HAROLD: I'm sorry it's so weird.

PETER: It's okay. Look, could you do me a favor? Could you maybe send me a picture every year? Like maybe on my birthday. I just wanna see what I'm gonna look like when I get old.

HAROLD: When's your birthday?

PETER: Last week. The fourteenth.

HAROLD: Oh. Happy Birthday. Yeah, I can do that.

PETER: Thanks.

HAROLD: Well, I should...uh... *(looking pointedly at MIRA)* Hm. I don't seem to remember where I put my *car keys*.

MIRA: I'll get 'em.

(MIRA runs off stage.)

HAROLD: Thanks. And how do I get back out of here?...I can't remember...

CLAIRE: Right at the stop sign. Left at the light. You'll see the signs for the highway.

HAROLD: Oh, that's right.

(MIRA runs back on carrying Harold's keys and a small white garment. She hands both to HAROLD.)

HAROLD: What's this?

MIRA: It's Peter's christening dress. I thought you might want it.

HAROLD: No...I can't...

MIRA: Sure you can.

HAROLD: Please don't do this to me.

MIRA: I want you to have it. It'll be good luck.

(HAROLD's eyes start to water. He holds the dress to his face and smells it.)

HAROLD: I...I have to go.

(PETER holds out his hand for Harold to shake. HAROLD starts to hug him instead, but changes his mind and shakes Peter's hand. HAROLD exits. PETER starts to cry. The women all rush toward him.)

PETER: Don't. I'm okay.

(They all move away. No one knows what to do.)

CLAIRE: He's a nice fellow.

MIRA: He really is.

PETER: Yeah.

PAIGE: Sorry I called him a dickhead.

PETER: S'okay.

(PETER takes a deep breath and looks at the women who are staring at him intently...he wants them to stop.)

PETER: Thanks, Moms.

CLAIRE: Oh, sure.

MIRA: No problem.

PETER: I know it was hard for you.

MIRA: It wasn't so bad.

PETER: He's a pretty good-looking guy. At least I know I'll look halfway decent when I'm old.

CLAIRE: He's younger than we are.

PETER: *(smiling)* Like I said... I need to get outta here. I wanna go for a ride or something.

CLAIRE: A ride! I almost forgot!

MIRA: What?

CLAIRE: Wait!

(CLAIRE retrieves the present that MIRA never opened and hands it to her.)

MIRA: What's this?

(MIRA opens the box and takes out two motorcycle helmets.)

MIRA: You bought me a motorcycle?

CLAIRE: I bought one bike for the both of us.

PETER: Go Mom!

PAIGE: Way cool.

CLAIRE: I want you to ride around the countryside with me. I want us to experience it together. It's really amazing.

(MIRA strokes a helmet and starts to cry. PETER signals to CLAIRE that they'll wait outside and leads PAIGE out.)

MIRA: That's the sweetest thing you've said or done in ten years.

CLAIRE: Is it? I didn't mean to wait so long.

(MIRA cries harder. CLAIRE goes to her and holds her.)

CLAIRE: I love you so damn much, Mira.

The phone rings. MIRA and CLAIRE look at one another. MIRA answers it.

MIRA: Hello?...This is she...Oh, hi!...Uh-huh...Yes, I'm still interested. Definitely...Great!...How's nine o'clock?...Okay...Great!...Thank you so much. Bye-bye.

(MIRA hangs up the phone, beaming.)

CLAIRE: Who was that?

MIRA: The Humane Society. I told them if no one adopted Slasher and Basher, that we would.

CLAIRE: You did?

MIRA: No one will take them, so I'm going to pick them up tomorrow morning.

CLAIRE: Really?! But Peter's allergic.

MIRA: Well, he'll just have to get shots. He's eighteen now and it's time for him to get over his silly fear of needles.

CLAIRE: You mean we're really gonna adopt two dogs?

MIRA: Yep! What do you think?

CLAIRE: I think you're beautiful.

MIRA: Oh, stop it.

CLAIRE: I'm gonna ravage you any second now.

MIRA: You are not.

CLAIRE: *(lunging for her)* I am.

(CLAIRE grabs the furry handcuffs and goes after MIRA. MIRA shrieks with delight and runs. CLAIRE catches up with MIRA, throws her onto the couch and pounces on top of her. CLAIRE snaps one cuff onto MIRA's wrist and the other onto her own, then kisses MIRA. They begin making out heavily. They roll around on the couch, they roll off of the couch, they roll across the floor...)

MIRA: I think you're having a mid-life crisis, Claire.

CLAIRE: No, you are.

(They continue making out while saying "No, you are." back and forth.)

PETER has gotten impatient and heads back inside to see what's keeping his moms. He enters unnoticed and sees what's keeping them. He smiles, then closes the door quietly and returns to PAIGE.)

PAIGE: Are they coming?

PETER: Um... They'll catch up. Let's go.

(Music starts: The Shangri-Las (or Bette Midler) singing "Leader of the Pack." PETER and PAIGE put on their helmets while CLAIRE and MIRA continue to wrestle around on the floor, trying to pull clothes off over the handcuffs, etc. PETER cranks up the bike. PAIGE climbs on and they take off as the lights dim and the music blares...)

BLACKOUT

                                        Curtain.

Proof

Made in the USA